—ᴍᴍ—

THIS JOURNAL BELONGS TO:

_____

_____

_____

—ᴍᴍ—

Progress always involves risk;
you can't steal second base and keep your foot on first.

—*mm*—

The Lord will either calm your storm
or allow it to rage while He calms you.

The golden age only comes to men
when they have forgotten gold.

— G. K. CHESTERTON

—*m*—

_____

_____

_____

_____

_____

_____

_____

_____

_____

_____

_____

_____

_____

_____

_____

_____

_____

_____

Do not wear yourself out to get rich;

have the wisdom to show restraint.

Cast but a glance at riches, and they are gone.

— PROVERBS 23:4, 5

A well-adjusted man is one
who can play golf as if it were a game.

We have not inherited the earth from our fathers;

we are borrowing it from our children.

— NATIVE AMERICAN PROVERB

—— *mm* ——

Many are the plans in a man's heart,
but it is the Lord's purpose that prevails.

— PROVERBS 19:21

Fear not that thy life shall come to an end,

but rather fear that it shall never have a beginning.

— JOHN HENRY NEWMAN

Angling may be said to be so like the mathematics
that it can never be fully learned.

— Izaak Walton, *The Compleat Angler*

The more I study nature,
the more I am amazed at the Creator.

— LOUIS PASTEUR

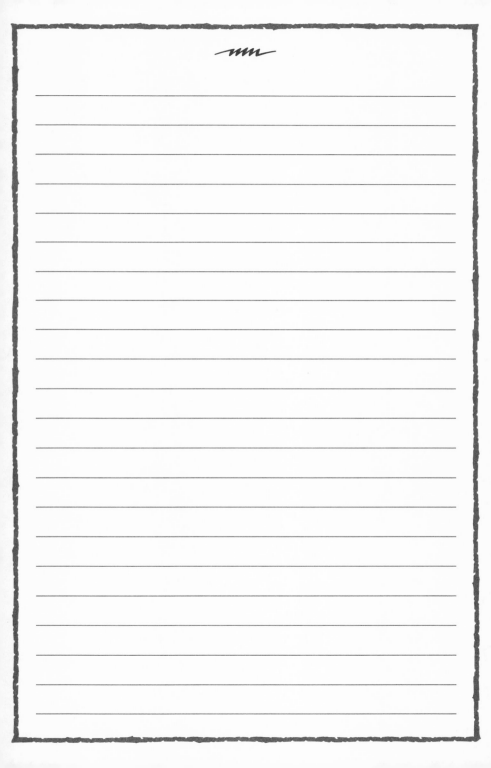

A ship in harbor is safe,
but that is not what ships are built for.

— JOHN SHEDD

A faithful man will be richly blessed.

— PROVERBS 28:20

One thought driven home is better than three left on base.

— JAMES LITER

If you are not guided by God,
you will be guided by someone or something else.

— ERIC LIDDELL

—*mm*—

You cannot teach a man anything;
you can only help him to find it for himself.

— GALILEO

Commit to the Lord whatever you do,

and your plans will succeed.

— Proverbs 16:3

_____

_____

_____

_____

_____

_____

_____

_____

_____

_____

_____

_____

_____

_____

_____

_____

_____

_____

_____

_____

To control his own ball, all alone without help or hindrance,
the golfer must first and last entirely control himself,
and himself only.

— JOHN STUART MARTIN

When we serve, we rule; when we give, we have;
when we surrender ourselves, we are victors.

— JOHN HENRY NEWMAN

Blessed is the man who finds wisdom,

the man who gains understanding.

— PROVERBS 3:13

We can easily forgive a child who is afraid of the dark;

the real tragedy of life is when men are afraid of the light.

— Plato

There are as good fish in the sea as ever came out of it.

— ENGLISH PROVERB

My great concern is not whether God is on our side,

my great concern is to be on God's side.

— ABRAHAM LINCOLN

He is a wise man who does not grieve for the things
which he has not, but rejoices for those which he has.

— EPICTETUS

_____

_____

_____

_____

_____

_____

_____

_____

_____

_____

_____

_____

_____

_____

_____

_____

_____

_____

_____

_____

_____

_____

_____

_____

A generous man will prosper;

he who refreshes others will himself be refreshed.

— PROVERBS 11:25

Things could be worse. Suppose your errors were counted
and published every day like those of a baseball player.

Success is to be measured not so much by the position that one has reached in life as by the obstacles which he has overcome.

— Booker T. Washington

An anxious heart weighs a man down,

but a kind word cheers him up.

— PROVERBS 12:25

*In golf as in life it's the follow through
that makes the difference.*

Do not follow where the path may lead.

Go instead where there is no path, and leave a trail.

Τrue peace is found by man in the depths of his own heart,

the dwelling place of God.

— JOHANN TAULER

Many men go fishing their entire lives
without knowing it is not fish they are after.

— Henry David Thoreau

We should all be concerned about the future
because we will all spend the rest of our lives there.

— CHARLES KETTERING